Cool Pets for Kids

# Rabbits, Mice, and Rats

**DAWN TITMUS**

PowerKiDS press

Published in 2019 by The Rosen
Publishing Group, Inc.
29 East 21st Street, New York, NY 10010

**Cataloging-in-Publication Data**

Names: Titmus, Dawn.
Title: Rabbits, mice, and rats / Dawn Titmus.
Description: New York : PowerKids Press, 2019. | Series: Cool pets for kids | Includes glossary and index
Identifiers: LCCN ISBN 9781538338063 (pbk.) | ISBN 9781538338056 (library bound) |
ISBN 9781538338070 (6 pack)
Subjects: LCSH: Rabbits--Juvenile literature. | Mice as pets -- Juvenile literature. | Rats as pets --
Juvenile literature.
Classification: LCC SF453.2 T58 2019 | DDC 636.932'2--dc23

Copyright © 2019

Text and editor: Dawn Titmus
Editorial Director: Lindsey Lowe
Children's Publisher: Anne O'Daly
Design Manager: Keith Davis
Picture Manager: Sophie Mortimer

Photo acknowledgements:
t=top, c=center, b=bottom, l=left, r=right
Interior: Alamy: Juniors Bildarchiv GmbH 7b, 8, Papilio 12-13, Tierfotogentur 17b, Neil Twigg 16,
Visual & Written SL 14-15; Dreamstime: Sergey Lavrentev 25t, Emilia Stasiak 27b; iStock: Argument 10, 11b,
Nick Biemans 14, James Brey 9b, 12, CreativeNature_nl 15, cynoclub 3, Image Source 4t, Jannoon028 7c,
kali9 13, nickpo 23t; Naturepl: Mark Taylor 24, 25b, Photoshot: Picture Alliance 17t, Lynn M. Stone 21t;
Shutterstock: Africa Studio 1c, 1r, 5t, 23b, 29bl, Andrew Burgess 4b, Shutterstock 19t, CKP1001 6r, Linn Currie
20, Maslov Dmitry 9t, George Dolgikh 7t, Jiang Hongyan 4-5, 5br, Hurst Photo 6l, Eric Isselee 18, 29t, Oksana
Kuzmina 29br, laurendotcom 21b, LiskaM 22, Photobac 10-11, 19b, schankz 27t, Emilia Stasiak 11t, Olesya
Tseytlin 5bl, Rudmer Zwerver 1l, 26.

Manufactured in the United States of America

CPSIA Compliance Information: Batch #CSPK18: For Further Information contact Rosen Publishing, New York,
New York at 1-800-237-9932.

# Contents

# Which Pet?

Rabbits, rats, and mice make fun and rewarding pets. Although they are not the most demanding animals, they all need some care and attention.

## Buying a Pet

Baby rabbits should stay with their mothers until they are about six to eight weeks old. You can bring baby mice home when they are five weeks old and rats when they are six weeks old. Buy directly from a breeder or a good pet store. Check out notices for these pets at the vet.

## Two's Company

Rabbits, rats, and mice all like company. They will be much happier living in a pair or as part of a group. Pets from the same litter make the best pairs. Keep two females or two males together and introduce them when they're young.

## Lifespans

Rats and mice do not live as long as dogs and cats. Mice live for one to two years, and rats live for about two to three years. Rabbits can live for up to 10 years.

## Rescue a Pet

Rescue centers and shelters are full of pets that need new homes. Think about giving a pet from a rescue center a forever home. Rescue centers can also give you advice about the best way to care for your new pet.

## The Right Pet for You?

☑ Do you have the space for a rabbit hutch or a cage for a mouse or rat?

☑ Do you have the time to care for your pet every day?

☑ Do you have the time for cleaning the hutch or cage every week?

☑ Are you willing to keep two or more pets together?

☑ Can your family afford the food costs and vet bills?

## Read On ...

Rabbits, rats, and mice are cute pets that are less demanding than some pets, but it is important to choose the right one. This book will help you to pick and care for your pet. Learn about six of the most popular types. Try your hand at making a fun zone for your pet. You will also find some fascinating facts about your furry friends!

# What You Will Need

All pets need some basic items, such as food and water bowls, bedding, some toys, and somewhere comfortable to live.

## What You Need

- ☑ Hutch, cage, or tank large enough for your pet.

- ☑ Food dish and water bottle the right size for your pet.

- ☑ Bedding and nesting materials, litter and litter box.

- ☑ Toys and treats.

- ☑ Pet carrier for rabbits.

- ☑ Exercise wheel for rats and mice.

## Food and Water

Your pet will need a shallow ceramic or metal food dish. They are easy to clean and cannot be chewed. A water bottle is better than a dish of water. It keeps the water clean and cannot be tipped over.

Water bottle

Food dish

## Housing Your Pet

You can keep rabbits outside in a hutch or playhouse. Rabbits can also be kept inside. Make a room in your home rabbit safe so you can let your pet out of its cage every day. You can keep rats and mice in wire cages or glass or plastic tanks. Make sure the tank has a tightly fitting mesh lid. Rats love to climb, and mice are escape artists!

## Pet Carrier

You'll need a pet carrier to take your rabbit on car journeys or to go to the vet. Rabbits can get very stressed in a moving vehicle. A nervous rabbit loose in a moving car may distract the driver. You can put pet mice and rats in a small box with holes cut in it for air.

## Litter Box

Rabbits and rats can be trained to use a litter box. Put the box in the area where there are usually droppings. Make sure the litter is safe for your pet. Clean out the litter box regularly.

# Housing Your Pet

**It's important to give your pet a comfortable home where it can live safely. Make sure you have what your pet needs before you bring it home.**

## Outside Rabbits

If you have to keep your rabbits outside, the hutch must be large enough for them to stand on their back legs, stretch, and hop around. A small wooden playhouse with a secure run attached is a good home for rabbits. Make sure it is secure from predators and in a shady spot. Give your pet a nesting box to sleep in, such as a small cardboard box lined with straw or hay.

## Inside Rabbits

Pet rabbits can happily live indoors. Make sure all the rooms it goes into are safe for your pet. Rabbits like to chew, so put electric cords out of the way. Indoor rabbits will need a private space, too, such as a cage. It should be five times the size of the rabbit and have a solid floor, not a wire one, to protect your pet's feet.

## Rat Homes

Rats need space to explore and exercise. Buy your pet the biggest cage you can. Put it on a raised surface away from drafts and heat sources, such as direct sun or radiators. Add bedding material and rat-safe litter. Provide a nesting box in the cage. A small cardboard box lined with soft paper tissue or paper towel makes a good nest.

## Playtime

All pets need to play to keep them fit and healthy. Chewing toys will keep your pet busy. Mice love to climb and play on a wheel. Rabbits like boxes and tunnels. Rats love to climb ladders and ropes. Give your pet time out of its hutch or cage every day to exercise and explore.

## Mice Homes

A wire cage or a 10-gallon (38-liter) glass or plastic tank is a good home for your pet. Use a tightly fitting mesh lid with a tank. The openings in a cage need to be 0.25 inch (6 mm) or less to prevent your mouse escaping. Put bedding on the floor, such as hardwood shavings, and provide a nesting box with strips of soft tissue or paper towel.

# Feeding Time

Rats, rabbits, and mice all have different food needs. Find out what food is best to give your pet and how much you need to feed it.

## Food for Rats

Feed your pet rat high-quality rodent pellets every day. Also give it washed fresh fruits and vegetables, such as small pieces of watermelon, banana, kale, and dandelion leaves. Make sure your pet has fresh water in its bottle every day.

## Feeding Rabbits

Give your rabbit plenty of hay to munch on every day. Also feed it some high-quality rabbit pellets. The amount of pellets to feed depends on your rabbit's weight. Rabbits like fresh fruit and vegetables, such as apples, cabbage, broccoli, celery, and carrots. They also love dandelion leaves. Give your pet fresh water every day. Rabbits can drink out of a dish, but a water bottle keeps the water clean. Check the bottle daily to make sure it is working.

## Food for Mice

Mice have tiny stomachs. Do not overfeed your pet or it will get fat! Give mice about a tablespoon of rodent pellets every day. Also feed them treats occasionally. Good treats for mice are a slice of apple, a few blueberries, tiny pieces of carrot, and broccoli. Make sure fruit and vegetables are washed well before you give them to your pet. Give your pet fresh water in a drinking bottle every day.

## Special Treats

There are lots of healthy treats that rats and mice like to eat. Low-fat, low-sugar cookies, breakfast cereal, whole-wheat bread, cooked pasta, and even pizza crust are all tasty treats. Never give your pet cheese or junk food such as candy, chocolate, or chips!

# Staying Healthy

Providing your pet with a clean home, fresh water, and the right kind of food will help keep it healthy. Check your pet every day for signs of sickness.

## Natural Behavior

All pets need something to do to stop them from getting bored and stressed. Give your pet plenty of toys and safe things to chew. Chewing is a natural behavior. Play with your pet every day and give it some time to exercise outside its cage or hutch.

## Fly Strike

Check your rabbit's rear end every day and clean it if it's dirty. Poop attracts flies, which lay eggs on the rabbit's body. The eggs hatch into maggots, which will burrow into a rabbit's body and make it very sick. If left untreated, fly strike (myiasis) can kill a rabbit. Take your rabbit to the vet if you think it has fly strike.

## Visits to the Vet

Check your pet's teeth and nails regularly. They can grow too long and cause health problems. Take your pet to the vet if its teeth or nails are too long. Rabbits need to be treated for worms, fleas, and ticks. They also need shots to prevent disease. Rats and mice do not need shots. Take them to the vet for a checkup every six months.

## A Clean Home

It's important for your pet's health to keep its home clean. Take out any soiled bedding, litter, and uneaten fresh food every day. Once a week, be sure to thoroughly clean out the cage and litter box. Use a pet-safe cleaner and rinse everything well. Replace the bedding and nesting material. Never use cedar or pine shavings for bedding. They can make your pet sick. Keep a little of the unsoiled bedding to put back in the cage so it still smells like home!

## Signs Your Pet May Be Sick

 Not eating or drinking.

 Staying in the nest during times it is usually active.

 Scaly patches on the skin.

 Runny eyes or nose, sneezing or wheezing.

 Diarrhea.

 Swellings on the body.

☑ Unsteadiness on the feet or falling over.

Take your pet to the vet if you think it is sick.

# In the Wild

Rats and mice live all over the world apart from Antarctica. Rabbits live in many parts of the world, except southern South America, Asia, and Antarctica.

## Rabbits, Rabbits!

In the wild, rabbits live in meadows, woods, forests, grasslands, deserts, and wetlands. Cottontail rabbits live in the Americas. Pet rabbits are descended from the European rabbit. It originally came from southwest Europe and northwest Africa. The European rabbit has been introduced to many parts of the world, such as Australia, New Zealand, and South America.

## Wild Mice

Mice are nocturnal—they are active at night. They do not have very good eyesight, but they have excellent hearing. In the wild, they build long underground burrows where they live. One male usually lives with several females and their young. Pet mice are domesticated forms of the house mouse rather than the field mouse.

## Rats of the World

Wild rats dig and live in underground burrows. A group of females and their young live in a burrow, where they build nest chambers. The burrow may be defended by one male, or there may be several males who share the burrow. Like mice, rats are nocturnal. Although rats and mice are related, they should never be kept in the same enclosure together.

# Himalayan Rabbit

The Himalayan rabbit is calm, friendly, and intelligent. It is one of the most popular rabbit breeds in the world.

## Where in the World?

Despite its name, the Himalayan rabbit probably comes from China, not the Himalayas. It has also been called the Chinese, Russian, and Egyptian rabbit. It was taken to England in the mid-1800s and arrived in the United States in the early 1900s.

The Himalayan rabbit has a soft, silky coat.

## Breed Profile

The Himalayan, or Himmie, has a white coat with colored markings on its nose, ears, feet and tail. These markings can be black, blue, chocolate, or lilac. The markings get darker in cold climates. The Himalayan weighs about 2.5 to 4.5 pounds (1 to 2 kg). It has a long, slender body and red eyes. The Himmie can live for up to 10 years.

## Looking After Me

The Himmie is a sociable rabbit that likes company. Keep two females, two males, or a neutered male and female together.

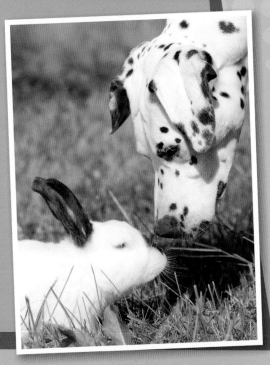

☑ Feed your pet quality hay and pellets, as well as plenty of fresh leaves and vegetables.

☑ The Himmie likes playtime—give your pet toys to play with.

# Holland Lop Rabbit

The Holland lop is a charming little rabbit with floppy ears. It likes affection and is easy to handle.

Holland lops are intelligent and docile.

## Where in the World?

The first person to breed Holland lops was a Dutchman, Adrian de Cock. He bred Holland lops in the 1950s. Holland lops were brought to the United States in 1976. They were recognized as a breed in the US in 1979.

## Breed Profile

The Holland lop has a broad body with a round head and full cheeks. As with all lop rabbits, it has long ears that hang either side of its head. It comes in a variety of colors, including gray, brown, black, and fawn. It weighs about 3.5 pounds (1.6 kg). The Holland lop lives for about 10 years.

## Looking After Me

The Holland lop is intelligent and can be trained to use a litter box. It is playful and active.

☑ Groom your Holland lop every day with a soft brush to keep its fur in good condition.

☑ Feed your pet plenty of high-quality hay and pellets, as well as fresh vegetables.

# Jersey Wooly Rabbit

## Where in the World?

The first person to breed the Jersey Wooly was Bonnie Seeley of New Jersey. She bred French Angoras with Netherlands Dwarfs. She introduced the Jersey Wooly to the American Rabbit Breeders Association in 1984. The Jersey Wooly was recognized as a breed in the United States in 1988.

The Jersey Wooly was originally bred to be a small pet rabbit. It has since become very popular as a show rabbit.

The Jersey Wooly is a small, gentle rabbit.

## Breed Profile

The Jersey Wooly rabbit has a short, compact body with small upright ears. It weighs about 3 pounds (1.4 kg). The wooly coat comes in a range of colors, including white, black, chocolate, blue, and tan. The Jersey Wooly lives for about 7 to 10 years.

## Looking After Me

Keep Jersey Woolies as house rabbits, rather than keeping them outside. Their small size makes them vulnerable to predators.

- ☑ The Jersey Wooly's short coat needs grooming about once a week.

- ☑ It likes lots of attention and playtime. Give it some rabbit-safe toys to play with.

# Standard Rat

The standard rat is a variety of pet rat. It is smaller than a wild rat and has a long body and a thick tail.

## Where in the World?

Pet rats are descended from the wild brown, or Norway, rat. Brown rats probably came from China originally. Today, brown rats live in all parts of the world except Antarctica.

The standard rat is the most common type of pet rat.

## Variety Profile

Pet rats are smaller than wild rats and have longer tails. The standard rat has a short, smooth, glossy coat. The coat can be one color or patterned. It has long, straight whiskers and round, upright ears. It is about 8 to 10 inches (20 to 25 cm) long from the nose to the base of the tail. Pet rats can live for about two to three years.

## Looking After Me

Pet rats are sociable animals. Keep a pair together to prevent loneliness and boredom.

☑ Give your pet a spacious cage with platforms at different levels and hammocks it can climb into.

☑ Feed your pet quality rodent pellets with small pieces of fresh fruit and vegetables.

# Rex Rat

This rat has a curly coat and whiskers. It is a popular pet variety, but always buy from a responsible breeder.

## Where in the World?

Rex rats were first bred in England in 1976. The first rex rats were brought to the United States in 1983.

The rex rat comes in a variety of colors.

## Variety Profile

The rex rat has a curly coat that can be long or short. The curls can be tight or wavy. Rex babies are born with a very curly coat. Males usually have more curls than females. After the first molt at six to seven weeks, the coat loses some of its curl. Rex rats can be one color or a mixture of colors.

## Looking After Me

Like all pet rats, the rex prefers to have the company of at least one other rat in the cage.

 Feed your pet high-quality rodent pellets with small pieces of fresh fruit and vegetables.

 A rex will start to get bald patches in its coat when it is about 18 months old.

# Standard Mouse

Pet mice come in many different varieties. The standard mouse has a glossy coat and black or pink eyes.

The standard mouse is the most common kind of pet mouse.

## Where in the World?

Pet mice are descended from the house mouse. Many different types exist today. The house mouse was originally from Europe and Asia north of the Himalayas and North Africa. It has been introduced to many parts of the world, such as the Americas, Australia, and southern Africa.

## Variety Profile

Pet mice range from hairless mice to long-haired Angora mice. Standard mice have a short, smooth coat. It can be one color, such as black or white, all over or be a mixture of colors. Pet mice are about 8 to 9 inches (20 to 23 cm) long from nose to tail tip. They usually live for about one to two years.

## Looking After Me

Mice are social animals and are best kept in pairs or groups. Keep two females or two males together or a neutered male and female pair.

 Give your pet a spacious cage with different levels for climbing.

 Feed your mouse small amounts of rodent pellets, seed mix, and fresh fruits and vegetables.

## Make It!
# Pet Fun Zone

Make a fun zone for your pet out of cardboard. Put some toys and treats inside, and your pet will love it!

### You Will Need:

Cardboard box(es)
Scissors
Newspaper
Tape
Paper towel tubes
Tissues or old phone book

**4** Put some paper towel tubes in the box for your pet to run through or push around.

**5** Add some tissues or an old phone book for your pet to shred.

**6** Hide some food treats or chew toys for your pet to find.

You could make a bigger fun zone by taping two or more boxes together.

**1** Use a box the right size for your pet. A shoe box is perfect for rats and mice. Rabbits need a box big enough for them to move around in.

**2** Remove any old tape or staples from the box. Ask an adult to cut doorways and windows in the box.

**3** Line the bottom of the box with pieces of cardboard or balled-up newspaper. Tape some cardboard pieces to the insides to create "rooms."

# Did You Know?

Rabbits, along with hares and pikas, belong to the group of animals called lagomorphs. Hares are the biggest animals of the group. Pikas are the smallest.

Rabbits have large eyes on either side of their head. They can see almost 360 degrees. They have a small blind spot in front of their face.

The Karni Mata Temple in India is famous for the 25,000 rats that live there. The rats are worshiped in the temple.

The American Rabbit Breeders Association (ARBA) recognizes 49 rabbit breeds.

Rats and mice belong to a large group of animals called rodents. The group includes squirrels, gerbils, beavers, gophers, and porcupines, among others.

Rats and mice have poor vision, but they have very good hearing and an excellent sense of smell.

A mouse can squeeze itself through a space the size of a dime.

Rats and mice use their tails to balance, communicate, and control their body temperature.

# Glossary

**burrow** (1) hole or tunnel in the ground that an animal makes for shelter. (2) to make a hole or tunnel in something.

**domesticated** living with people.

**flea** very small biting insect that lives on animals.

**hammock** type of bed made of fabric that clips to the cage and hangs free.

**litter** (1) dry material placed in a litter box. (2) group of young animals born at the same time to the same mother.

**maggot** young form of a fly that looks like a small worm.

**molt** lose a covering of skin or hair to make way for new growth.

**neutered** refers to an animal that has had its sex organs removed so it cannot produce young.

**nocturnal** active at night.

**pellet** small hard ball of food for animals.

**predator** animal that kills other animals for food.

**rodent** small animal such as a rat or mouse that has sharp front teeth.

**tick** very small insect that attaches itself to a larger animal and feeds on it.

**vaccination** treatment with a substance, called a vaccine, to protect against a particular disease.

**vulnerable** open to attack or injury, easily harmed or injured.

**whiskers** long, thin hairs that grow near the mouth of some animals.

**worm** animal that lives in the stomachs of animals and people.

# Further Resources

## Books

**Beck, Angela.**
*Rabbits: Keeping and Caring for Your Pet.* Enslow Publishers, 2013.

**Foran, Jill and Katie Gillespie.**
*Rabbit (Caring for My Pet).* AV2 by Weigl, 2014.

**Jeffrey, Laura S.**
*Choosing a Hamster, Gerbil, Guinea Pig, Rabbit, Ferret, Mouse, or Rat: How to Choose and Care for a Small Mammal (American Humane Association Pet Care).* Enslow Publishers, 2013.

## Websites

Due to the changing nature of Internet links, PowerKids Press has developed an online list of websites related to the subject of this book. This site is updated regularly. Please use this link to access the list:

www.powerkidslinks.com/cpfk/rabbits

# Index